Dear Nijel,
Thank you for your
support
Malka

BIRDS WITHOUT SKY

Poems from exile

MALKA AL-HADDAD

I extend my heartfelt gratitude

to all my English friends that protected me

in their warm hearts, considered my papers,

saturated with love

Malka

My home is gone
My heart is broken
My tears said:
write a book

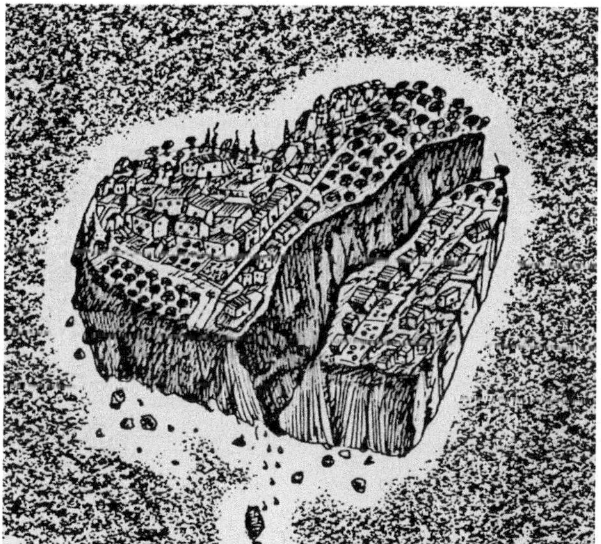

Published by Ludensian Books

First published in Great Britain in 2018

Paperback ISBN: 978-0-9554939-9-7

British Library Cataloguing in Publication Data
A CIP catalogue record for this book can be obtained from the British Library.

Cover design: London Tags

Edited by: Richard Byrt

Illustrations by: Tethkar Al-Haddad (pages viii,10, 16, 24, 31, 40, 46, 58, 65, 76, 81, 93)

George Sfougaras (pages 11, 12, 15, 23, 28, 29, 32, 33, 34, 35, 36, 38, 41, 42, 43, 44, 45, 47, 48, 51, 54, 57, 59, 61, 62, 63, 69, 73, 77, 85, 87, 89, 90)

Produced and distributed by:

HARRIMAN HOUSE LTD

18 College Street, Petersfield, GU31 4AD, UK
Tel: +44 (0)1730 233870

www.harriman-house.com

CONTENTS

Acknowledgements

I want to say a big thank you to all my wonderful British friends in Leicester, Birmingham and Lincolnshire, who gave me a chance to feel that there is a safe and peaceful life in this country.

Many friends have helped me to publish my poetry book. Thank you to you all. My particular thanks and acknowledgements to:

Richard Byrt, for your comments and suggestions and for editing this collection. George Sfrougaras and Tethkar Al-Haddad for your wonderful illustrations which breathe new life into my poems. Carol Leeming, for your analysis of my poems.

London Tags, for the cover design.

Sarah Taal, for support and inspiration; and Kate Mitchell, for helping me to make a collection of my poems after they were dispersed. Jenny Hibberd for helping with my final review before publication, and for your music. Kathleen Bell, Emma Lee and Siobhan Logan, Editors, and Five Leaves Publications; Emma Lee and Ambrose Musiyiwa, Editors, and Dahlia Publishing Ltd., for your support and encouragement.

Credits

"Children of War" was previously published in Over Land, Over Sea, Poems for Those Seeking Refuge, Nottingham: Five Leaves Publications; and in British Pensioner, Ed. 101, Winter, 2016/17.

"Leicester" and "Homeland" were previously published in: Welcome to Leicester, Poems about the City, Leicester: Dahlia Publishing, Ltd.

"I'm Human" was previously published in: Financial Rhymes for Financial Times, Leicester: The People's Arts and Bradgate Writers Combined Collective, 2017 (Produced by Peter Buckley).

"Leicester" and "Homeland" were nominated for the Pushcart Prize, 2016.

A pamphlet consisting of the first section of this collection was longlisted for the Cinnamon Press Poetry Pamphlet Competition, 2017.

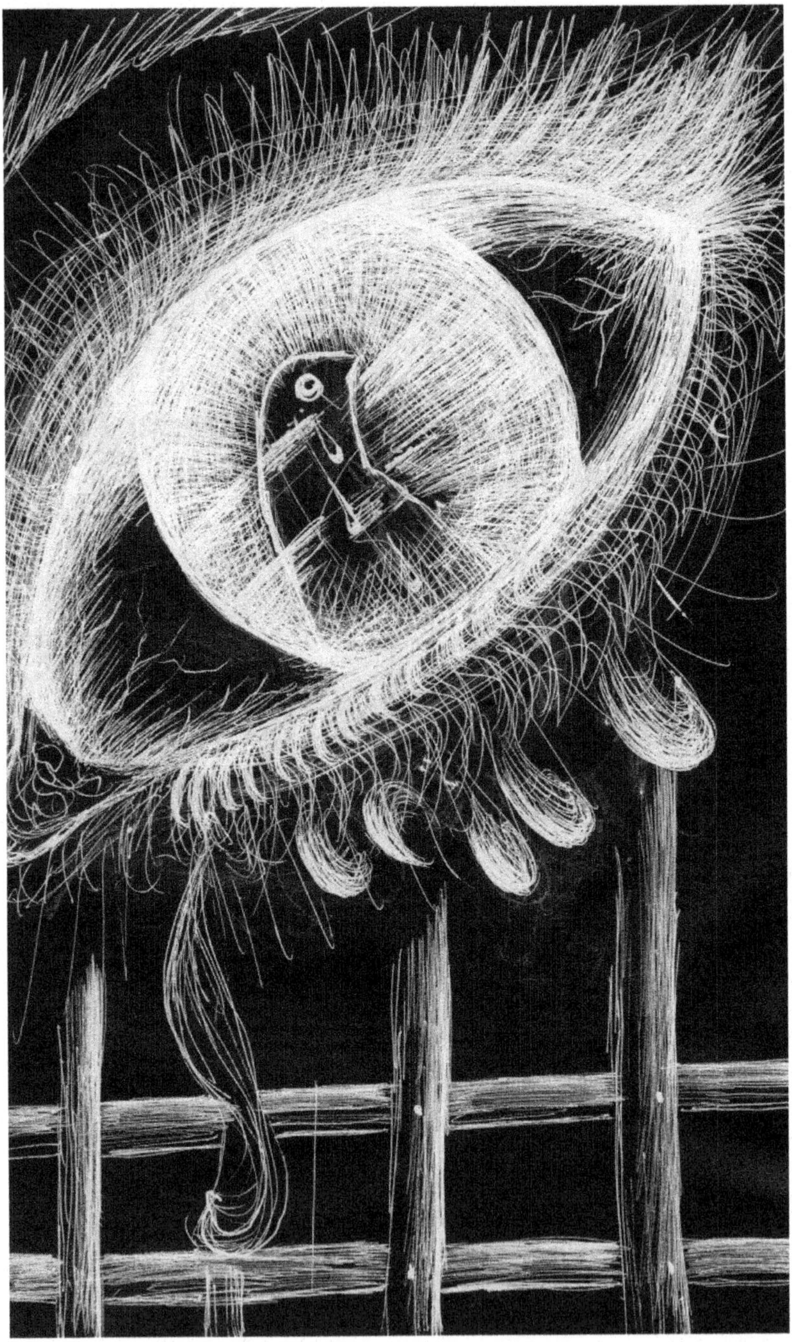

Introduction

I am Malka, a person without papers, a bird without sky. In my poems, I visualize refugees as birds who are forced to flee, and give up everything for liberty. Birds symbolize the fragility of freedom in non-democratic countries. I stand and fight with them, for freedom.

I grew up in Iraq, in an artistic family. My father and older sisters are well known artists. My parents are loving and passionate, and taught me to be emotional and imaginative, free, open and genuine; to be strong and independent and get a good education; above all, to protect my freedom. I learned from them, that love is the most beautiful thing in life, despite living and facing obstacles in a very strict religious city and old traditional society.

After 2003, the Triangle of Death visited my beautiful country. I lost my homeland to invasion by the US, to ISIS and to religions which have a political agenda. I felt I no longer belonged to society and the culture of my wonderful country had collapsed.

My father taught me that freedom is not only to do what we want; that real freedom is to do what we should do. Without freedom, life is extinct. This inspires me to be responsible towards others, help and support those in need, and responsible towards our society, protecting our rights and our great culture. So, I couldn't be silent when I saw human rights violations, discrimination, corruption and sectarian conflict. I became angry and fought back: as a human rights activist, I published critical articles, and spoke publicly. I established the Women's Centre for Arts and Culture. These activities led me to be victimized in my homeland. I was forced into exile. It is not easy to be torn from the country and the people that you love and trust. I cannot change the world, but I can speak out through my poetry and through continuing my human rights work from here. Writing poetry helps me to release something previously unknown, to make it visible and tangible. I hope it gives the reader a perception about the experience of being a refugee from a country ripped apart by war. I hope it helps to bring people together.

Malka al-Haddad – United Kingdom, October 2017.

FOREWORD

Malka al Haddad's collection of poems, to echo her exquisite metaphor in the title, and throughout her writing, are winged; they literally take flight off the page. In some of her shorter poems there is a tautness that conveys great depths of emotion with a grave economy. While some of the longer poems are able to simultaneously condemn, lament and exclaim angrily, and exult with stunning lyrical beauty.

These poems, therefore, are like bittersweet love songs; the whole work, a movement of melancholia, ire, joy of life and love, as they skilfully conjoin castigation of war, sad memories of loss, familial longing, geo-political rape of homeland, the fickle nature of a lover's heart or statelessness – a refugee's fate.

This deft weaving of al Haddad's poetry does not seem defeatist, on the contrary, particular poems about London and Leicester feature strongly, with a sense of ebullient, emergent hope, to suggest a welcome start to a new life. However, in the midst of reveries e.g. say of nature in a new home, ever present are the felt absences of loved ones, along with a fondly remembered homeland before war, death and destruction. This often frames a refugee's daily experience and these poems merely give us readers a fleeting glimpse.

As I have mentioned above, birds figure prominently as a metaphor for refugees: 'birds without sky.' Just three words used only to evoke such immense human suffering. I liked the use of short addressed letters e.g. a superb line from al Haddad's poem She And He: 'And moon wrote my body its letters'; another is the letter to Trump, with its assertion and centring of a pre-eminent Muslim identity. This underscores the importance of the actual act of writing. To speak truth to power as a way to combat and transcend intersectional oppression, both personal and political, is, I think, highlighted in the phrase in the first poem in the collection by way of personification: 'My tears said: write a book'.

I warmly commend this book for its beauty and enduring strong soulful humanity.

Carol Leeming, FRSA,
28th June 2017

Poems

I'm Human

I'm from a country at war
I'm from a country that's bleeding
A country of anger
And revolutions
A country of martyrs,
I'm from a country once called Mesopotamia
I'm from the land of black gold
I'm from the richest land on the earth
I'm from the land of sunshine on a golden desert.

I'm from there
But I'm not there.

I had beautiful dreams
I had friends, brothers, sisters, sweet parents and pink hopes.
I had green gardens, tall palms and olive trees
I had a warm winter
Blue rivers
Red flowers
I was born on land before the crossing of swords on the body
Turned it into a banquet table

Before Bush and Blair turned our rivers to blood
Then they donated millions of tents instead of roofs for our houses

The rain has died in my homeland.

They left graves in the green grass in our fields.
Only cacti remain laughing in the barren desert.
The sun has become ashamed behind the clouds,
Where is God?
Has even God become a refugee in His land?
Where is our ancient law?
Has even this been stolen?

No choice,
I crossed the seas of death.
Waves of grief have led me here
To the land of my usurpers in an old and narrow shelter.

No job
no identification
no dignity.

Victims cannot judge their executioner…

I now speak in two languages, but I have forgotten in which one
I used to dream

I have learned all the words to take,
The lexicon apart for one noun's sake
The compound I must make:
Homeland.

No choice I came here.

I'm here
But I'm not here.

You are a refugee and
Your choice is not your choice

But remember...
I'm human
I'm human

Children of War

Every child in my land suffers torment of wars.

Every child in my land suckles milk mixed with fear.

I ache, ache from the gun at my side:
your gift, Father, the day before they killed you.

You told me your gun would be my best friend.
It has been with me each day and each night. And still

Every child in my land suffers torrents of wars.

Every child in my land suckles milk mixed with fear.

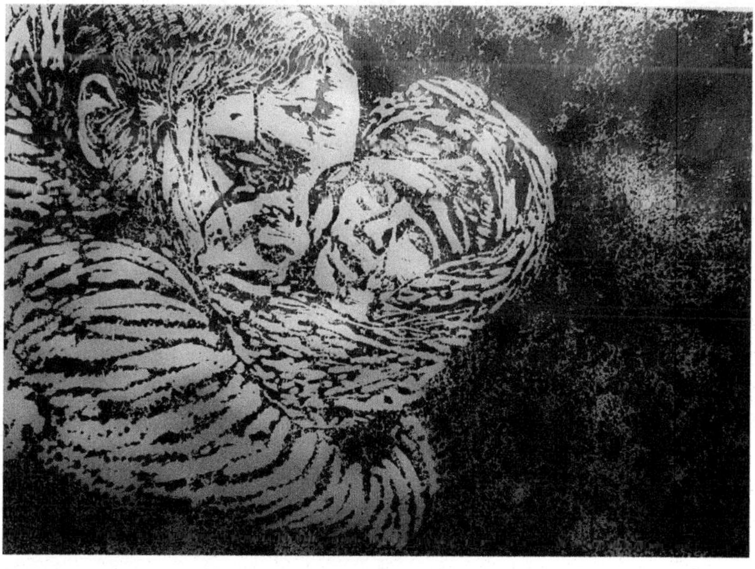

Gift

There is a bullet in my writing.
It is a small gift from the gun you left in my home,
To remind you

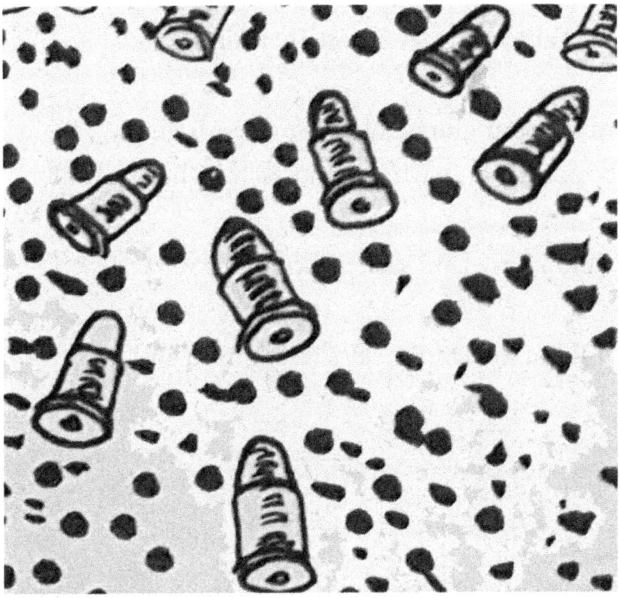

Schizophrenia

We are poets
Who practise the hobby of death with silence.

Who draw the map of their death with concentration and bravery.
Who cuddled their bullets with smiles on their lips thirsty for love.
Who hid their kisses in pores of their skin since the first war announced their names in exclusion lists,
Made necklaces from shrapnel when the war ended in Autumn.

We are poets
Who couldn't stifle secrets in our throat

Who ran from time of betrayals
Towards a sadness for homeland
Raped by pigs and thieves

We are poets,
Whose homeland has shrieked
And our ink expanded

We are poets,
Who search among rocks and bombs
For what is left of wars and stabbed friends,

We are poets,
Who love our sweethearts so dear to us,

Killed in daylight, left bleeding in dark night.

We are forsaken,
Homeless,
Stateless,
Rebellious,
Dreamers;
We are madness.
We write our love stories in bars of tormentors on old café tables
Defying oblivion on our papers

We are poets,
Our emptiness filled with lost dreams.

We are poets,
Who sit in train stations without tickets
Walk without end on unknown roads, with death our invisible muzzle

We are poets,
Who sell flowers from time of ashes.

We are poets,
drawing dreams with words,
our imagination creates happiness, love, peace,
homes for people.
But we are still homeless.

We are poet,
And our exile is pubs and poems.

American invasion

There is oil in your pocket
And there is blood in my blood
I look for a shower
To wash wars off me
I'm still searching
searching
searching

MONTH OF FAREWELL

Dear December!
Please be the last month of pain
Be the last page in the book of letdowns
Be the last train in years of waiting
Be the last station of Farewell
Please, my dear, give me a Gentle Goodbye as there isn't space in my heart for
another wound
Please, be wonderful and make our dreams come true.

December and Love

Love does not begin only when music of rain begins

And Poetry always comes
With the rain.

If December comes
All longing, yen, and nostalgia besiege me

I ask... ask for your eyes, hands, every cloud every night, and stars

And your beautiful face always comes with rain, rain, rain...

What I do among lightning ignites in my heart and expects Jesus

December besieges me with love
In everywhere, I look for your hands, voice, shoulder, eyes...

When my baby comes, the trees will forget all the sorrows of autumn
What beautiful exile if we were together
What beautiful rain when our hands clasp each other.

Come baby and let our soul melt in season love
Let me reorder stars on your fingers
Let me express what wine glass thinks about your beautiful lips

and how Jesus's wine
rebirths on your breast
fire in month of snow...
month of love...
month of dreams…
month of birth…

Letter to Santa

Dear Santa,
When you arrive on Christmas Eve could you please bring back our dreams that
have been stolen
My school...
my friends...
that became ashes under fire,

The roof of our house,
The smell of Mum and Dad,

Why they left me without goodbye.
There was a green garden, a Ferris wheel,
ice cream vans,
shadow of lovers.

Nothing left for us...
only the stench of death.

Santa – how can you find the smile of childhood
that has been buried underground
without shrouds
without a funeral
without a farewell?

Please Santa take back your precious gifts and give me back only my home and
peace.

Dear Santa,
sorry that your children are now not here any more
Sorry Santa
your children have become men in wartime…
and their toys are guns and their ecstasy is the smell of gunpowder

Bird and Dream

I set up my decoration,
prepared my love poems for her blue eyes.
Lit candles,
Violin and orchid's perfume everywhere...
I tell Snowman
Wait... Wait, don't melt your heart, she is coming
I think the green grass is jealous of me and perhaps tried to impede her!

The time has flown and gone,
My cigarettes burned with my heart
Burned... Burned
Then she didn't come!

I drank her glass of wine and smashed it,
covered the mirror to avoid her imagined face

In the night, I opened all my curtains and windows...
no secrets in my heart except what I waited for and lost

I said I will forget that I wrote adoring poetry for her
And I will repeat the order of the evening to fit with my disappointment and her
absence
Then I read the chapter on distant planets
And story of dreams of the poor lovers,
Then I realize I'm one of the crazy folk who try to hunt planets,

I said I will not write a poem for her again;
I will write for forgetfulness of her offences.
Then I wrote this poem!

Homeland

We are citizens without a homeland,
Hunted like birds without sky,
Taught how to cut our wings,
Cage our love inside us,
Love is sin - not forgiven,
Freedom of speech is shame,
We are immigrants on all maps without addresses,
Travellers, paperless, without passport,
Bodies without coffins,
We are slaves of time,
Sell us all, governor, and get the price,
Here, here, stop your journey here,
stop your suffering, exile and grief.
England has revealed to us what it means:
love, peace and homeland.

Leicester

You are a legend of cities.
You embody all the glories of ages.
My sweetest sparrow, my precious harp.
My tears splattered my cheeks as I travelled in exile.
But here, I dream of violets, remember perfumes,
birds soaring through clouds.
Your throne is still engraved like royal mirrors
of all times and places.
Your love still grows within your Roman walls.
You light a flame of love in my heart which will never fade.
Still your tune dances in my veins.

How I longed for such a home
like Summer waits for rain.
People see me as a refugee.
But I am a free bird, nestling in your grass.
I have nothing, only love and rain, but I'm richest
under your warm heart, drawing me to your depths.
In the fire of your love, even my blood becomes wine.

You and me are love until deep sleep, sleep-moon.
You are all letters, all language.
You are the end, the start of my journey.

Big Love in a Small City

Reading... Reading...
everywhere in Leicester
Over Land Over Sea...
Leicester is reading its love, its peace, its hopes and solidarity

Read… Read till we make our letters like light stars

Read… Read of our fearless
                                        Foxes' winners

Read… Read for the welcoming of refugees…
                                        for a child's smile…

Read… Read till we make our words taste like red wine

Read…Read till we see lovers cuddling and melting
                                        till we hear a lover's guitar touch all hearts

Read… Read this is a multicultural town,
                                        we are all shades of black, white and brown

Read... Read we are all one, Jews, Muslims and Christians

Read… Read, the shining sun
                                        is coming to our courtyard
                                        till we shine together, you and I

Read... Read till our dreams inspire our souls for a new dawn

Read… Read, we are the life blood of King Richard!

Read… Read till the moon sleeps on our rhymes...

Heartbroken

The most dangerous
of those thieves,
who steal hearts
loaded with the innocence
and purity of love
and then return them to us
in ruins...

Love and Fair

In the heart
of every woman
a small cave
hides memories, nostalgia
for the someone
departed from her world
she visits now and then
even though she's living with
another love.

War

Wars are programmable
in the minds
before using
arms...

Pain of Memory

remain
your facial features
sleeping
in my heart
wake up
whenever glimpsed
stranger carries
your profiles

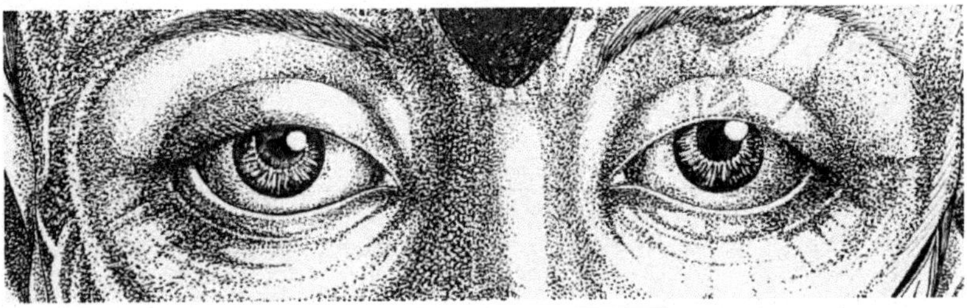

Promise

You promised me
between us
will be eternal.
And I forgot to ask you:
is it your love or my pain?

WELL MIND

To everything
there is arms…
and arms of mind
is to bear with ignorance.

DEPARTED

You left sadness
in palaces.
Sadness
walking
instead of my feet

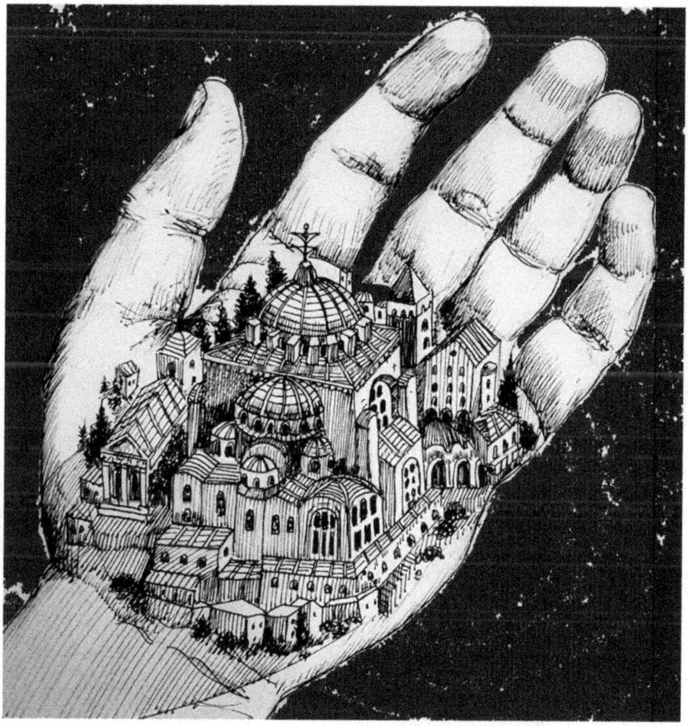

Women in Trees

Oh highness tree,
do not care,
strengthen your roots,
expand your leaves,
keep going on your elevation.

Cuddle sun rays.
Call your birds.
All of them need you.

Their dreams have dangled their secrets and stories on your branches.
All seasons from you and to you.
How much storms have challenged you.
How they wished to arrest your birds.
Their hands are exhausted.
Their axes have broken.
But you stayed as you are, proud.

Disappointment

I've held my coffin
on my shoulder
and walked in the funeral of my dreams

A BIRD IS NOT A STONE

Go away whenever you want.
And peace be upon you wherever you depart.
No longing,
sipping the rain.
And no heart still waiting for you.
It's a soul.

Only in the kingdom of exile
will you be resurrected.
Dialogue with blossom, clouds
soaring with sikal birds
where sails oblivion,
rippling on the wings of the wind
and blue waves
and dreams of snow white.

Sleep until dusk on green grass
and violet flowers
in amaryllis morning. No limits.
No fences can obscure,
she has been created for love and peace.
Her love is violins playing.

Oh Man, whose breathing from ancient times
who stole flowers all those years ago,
who worships at the altar of the flesh
no longer in this endless heart.

Go away.
Go away.
She screams from the silent coffin,
her delicate flowers
cannot be covered by tribal ritual.
Selfish Man,
who cannot understand her even once.
She is delicate as snow
Below the equator's torture,
Enough.
Enough.

Absent

you are
very distant
but I see you here all the time

She and He

She said:
Do not fatigue horse's back
Pride body has raped
My hankering
My heart swimming in the kingdom of the soul and in sail's exile.
We are both body:
You are the body of the consumer
And I'm the embalmer of the body
You are departing
You are transitory.

And moon wrote my body its letters,
And all lovers' dreams on my lips.
On my breast
The ice committed suicide.

RAPE

They said, "we will liberate you",
then they raped us.
My head in Baghdad.
My neck in Fallujah.
My arms in Mosul.
My legs in Tikrit.
My eyes in Basra.
Then when I ran away to Churchill,
he desired every part
every part
of my body.

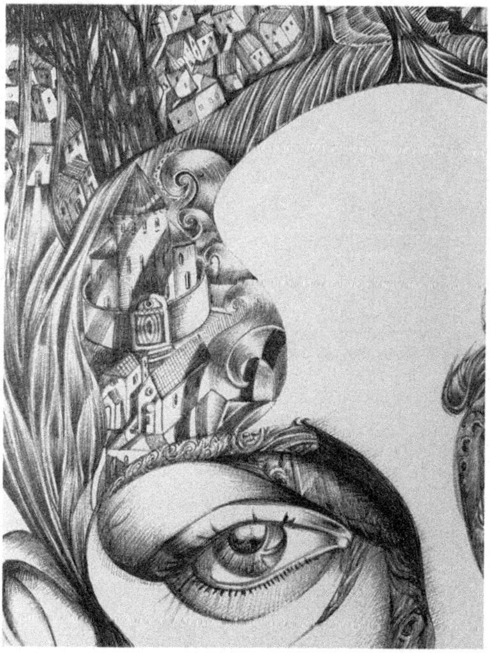

Let the Storm Break

Love is yearning
for you secretly
And you kill
me overtly.

Dark

There was no morning
In that night you left me.
Please, can you bring back my eyes

Longing

Even my dreams
don't have you.
So it's a great consolation
you're there
in my poems.

Butterfly

I was a butterfly.
But your scissors
cut off
my wings.

FOREVER

How can you kill
the love
after bleeding
on these pages

Knife in my Side

From the heart of the storm
                        from the line of fire
Engraved my words,
                        nostalgia, in my heart
Tears wash me, shaking
                        thought, choked up in my soul
And under black sky a thousand walls
                        collapse.

Look for your face
Look for your hand

And your voice drifting away, away
                        lost in the mirage of eternity
scatters under mirrors. Embers
                        dissolve, dissolve like rains.

Oh my homeland
Oh my homeland

Your images live in mine:
                        swimming in my veins
                        breathing from my lung
                        drinking from my heart.

Planting whole planets,
Plants of wheat, conch and oyster
                        planting a knife in my side.

Distant star

She alone is the one I go to in each and every dream...

My Mum.
Miss you.

Liberation from the Lie

Olive branch and Noah's doves are laments
and Mary's plaits on the slaughtered body.
The smell of secrets
arise over the brow of the silver moon.
Narrate that once upon a time
there was a house, a girl, a cradle.

It was there...
shadow of two lovers
It was there…
scarf and promise.

It was there ...
then it became
fire, tomb, coals…
intrigue, subdue and manacle.

Wounds pity them. Poems
reverberate shame,
wrap our grandmother
and children of yesterday –
no longer children.

So tell her to close her eyes,
falsely it has become all her stories
as the Lord of the House has sold his dwelling
and Moses chokes on his stick.

And flood has swallowed Noah's Ark

and sea fish have
habitual gyrations.

Death among the alleys
is no longer strange.
It strolls under cover,
Walks under cover.

Soul Killer

Body killer.
Visible by his act.

But people do not know
you kill my soul.

Memories are all you left me.

Pawns in the Game

The sky turns scarlet
when doves disappear
and aircraft appear.
Our homes:
Lines for blood-splattered clothes.

Every moment
makes us
martyrs,
prisoners,
orphans,
immigrants.

Palm trees walk
on crutches,
reel, then die.
No wheat. Drought.
Only grief trees grow.
Grow without rain.

Black crows caw.
Caw above houses
no longer
with walls.
Birds of high mountains
have gone
beyond the sea.

Look for
New meaning.
New life.
New truth.
We are ships without sails.
Between the sea
and the sea,
looking for waves, which
dislocate the depth of my memory.
Still those distant cities stick in my memory
Cities of fear, blood and wailing

We are diaspora.
Home and exile,
The same face,
same sword,
same destiny.

Our life under siege.
Siege is waiting.
Waiting on ladders
sloping in the centre
of storm.

We are immigrants
into the unknown.
Prisoners planting
hope behind fences.

We are alone.
Alone. In a jungle.
Without shade.

We are injured horses.
Our hope is the bullet of mercy.
We are ships without sails.
We are pawns in the game.
We are pawns in the game.

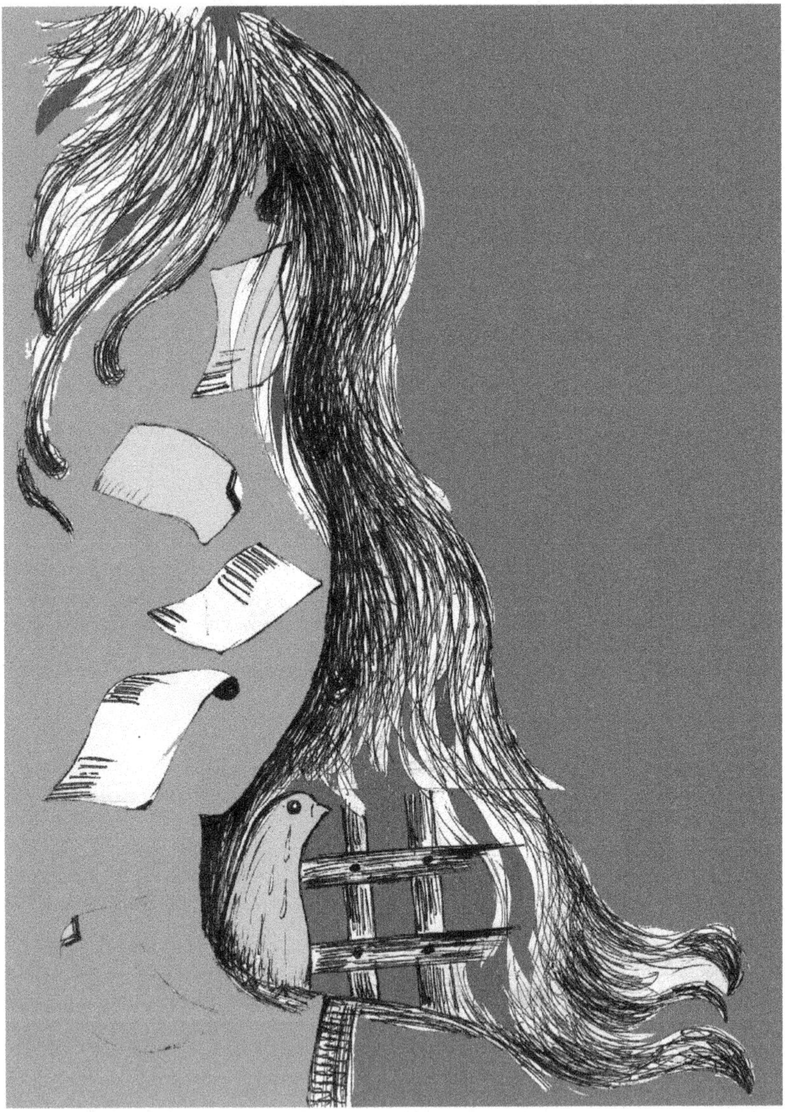

The Agony of Memory

The night.
Infinite.
Unforgettable
songs.
Glasses of wine
reflecting
memories.

And longing for someone.

City of Love

London
peace be upon you
Your love
bigger than
foolish storm
wanted to hide you.

Our love song's stars
in the night would protect you,
We are all lovers beside you,
Warm be the sun that shines on you.

Soft heart is you
Great bridge is you
Ancient walls are you
World eye is you.

Big Ben...
Big Ben
ring ring
sing sing
All of us
sacrifice
For you.

Tell black crow
Rough hand
Cannot touch
Smooth heart.

CHERISH

She likes paddling kayak
And I have been wearing the sea all the time

ARGYLL FOREST

By blue seas
Where white sailboats challenge dancing waves,
Where tall trees
Embrace singing birds,
Where two lovers cultivate green shrubbery,

Where my heart
Aches to get back something.
Something has gone...
Something I lack
Maybe home.
Maybe hope.
Maybe a friend.
Maybe forgetfulness.
Maybe myself.

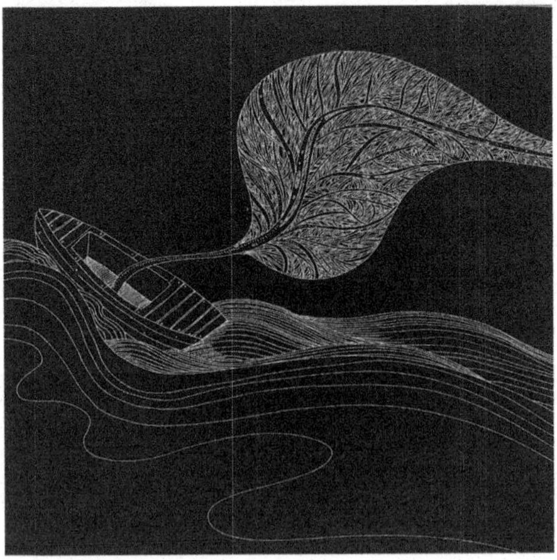

Love

Love is to give
Because you want,
Not because I want.

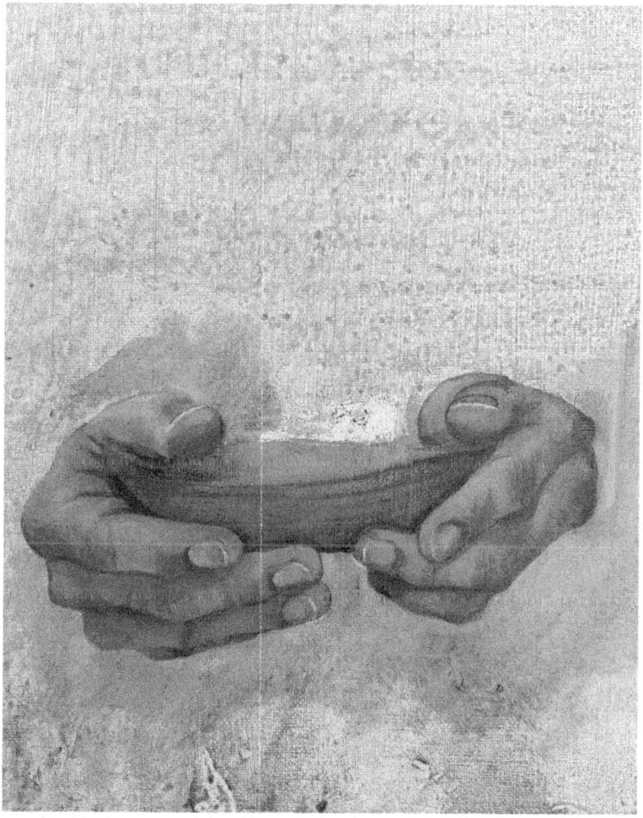

Louth

Louth is the heart of love
Where my dreams reach the sky
Where the rain quenches my thirst
Where my mind finds tranquillity
Where the high trees shadow my sadness
Where my lips taste smiles and laughter

Here and there
Lost and found
Dark and light

Irish angel

You are four years of tears.
You smell like a dream,
Like love,
Like birth,
Like death.

Painting Unique Love

Art is a part of our soul
Lines, colours and shapes,
Textures, values and spaces
Guide us to swim in a sparkling sea of imagination
Into the ancient past and green present
Reaching distant stars.
It is our own personal healing…
Come and walk beside art,
Come to inspire your mind
To live here out loud,
Come to the new walks
To create your meditation through art
And make your soul grow, for inner beauty.

Each creation showcases different personal journeys,
Do not let them go.
All you can imagine through them is real.
This is your own art.
Art is the truth that is revealed to us
And realizes the invisible,
Giving wings to fly
Among lines, colours and shapes,
Global arts taste sweet.

Paintings coming to you from across the world,
Touching your heart

Opening your mind
Uniting our different backgrounds
Until it mixes our bare colours:
Black, white or brown
Paints
Unique love.

Challenge

And I heard her say,
Leave me alone.
But love is not afraid of her,
So, let us share our wars.

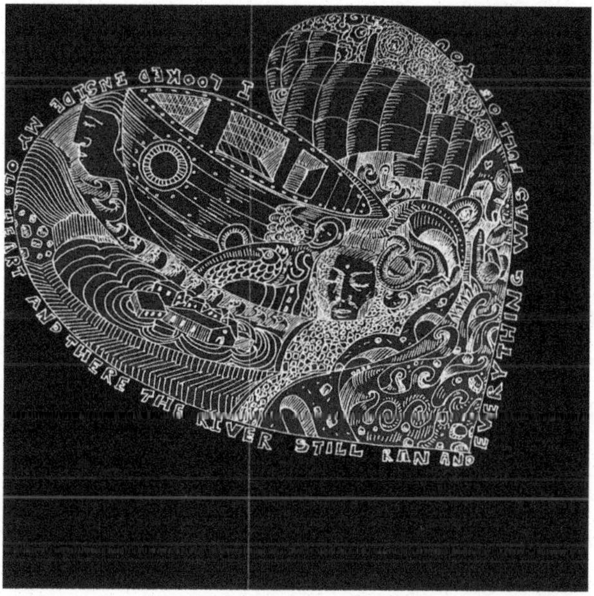

Release

The river running free,
sails dancing in the sea,
hazel on the trees,
butterflies sheltered by the wind,
tercel bird out in the sky,
ruffling clouds' hair with his beak
unfurls his wings
like a lance
takes flight …
dove flies high, and higher…
to extend an olive branch of Peace.
New dawn
New life
New eyes…

She sat down on the rear corner bench.
There was room for someone close and far,
Someone who can plant darkness and light,
Someone who can remove the sword, release her heart
that clings to the knife in her side.
Someone who, might one day,
feel what she lost, so it is found.

To Bush and Blair

Not our fault. We were born in barracks built by you,
planted our flowers in military helmets
looking for smell's love of ruin,
made nests on trees of Autumn.
Your death caught us everywhere.

The children of Iraq's dreams
are not the dreamless ones.

No hand for peace, a thousand hands for bombing, killing, deportation

And still you want more.
You made Iraq outside Iraq.
Your soldiers broke down our homes, dreams, ambition,
humiliated our men, disgraced our women.
Your war killed our peace.
You stole all our hope.
The name of God and peace kills every day.
And still you want more.

We run towards fate unknown.
Then you face us, judge us, plunder us,
as you did when you came to my country.
Such a sheep-gathering on the deck.
Where do I begin, where does it end?
All I have in exile is pen and paper.

You are a torturer. We know you force water.

We left everything for you.
We want only the return of our peace.

Friend

A friend is someone who
precedes your question before your tears

Waiting at the Door

I cannot celebrate Eid.
I cannot forget my mother's face,
or wonder if she still waits, waits for me at the door.

I am a wandering bird without feathers.
My homeland gone. Far, far from my family.
Cast away from a home where I cannot reside.

Boat migrants die. No one remembers.
I die every day. Nobody knows.
Friends, family, neighbours back home, I want you to know,
One day, together we will be heard.

Longing

When I miss my homeland
I smell my poems
And I weep.

A Small Bird and the Home Office

In my tight shelter
My tears, fear pulls me apart:
A woman who writes her freedom on raindrops

Who drew a home on the cloth pillowcase that she lost

And another who watches me from behind closed windows
And her killing shout points it towards me between
A diaspora of madness.
Or the last farewell train,
A difficult balance:
Exchange a dream for a nightmare
Exile for exile

Fear and love
War and peace
May and me

Where is our path ?

Fat of the Land

O land that took my heart
I planted my blood on you
Please grow love
Or jasmine flowers
Grow hope or voice's lovers
Spread wheat or peace
Not tombs or graves
No screaming or wailing

O land punctured with shrapnel
O sky of my land
Is there air to breathe
Is there hope to dream
Is there roof to sleep
Is there morning without bullets penetrating pores of my skin
Is there memory of childhood smile?

O land punctured with shrapnel
Where war plans shadow us
Where Bush and Blair sold us as firewood for their war game

Leaders of the West!
Warmongers,
Where is my home, that you snatched from us?
Like skinning sheep,
You let our blood flow over more than our oil
Rapists, occupiers,

What have you done to our dreams?
How much of our bread have you stolen?
What have you left us?
Let up
Let up
Let me carry my poems and my coffin
Before they get stolen.
Liars, mutilators,
Where is our freedom?
Voiceless because I dither so much

Painful my voice. Lonely strings playing.
Our cities are no longer for us.
The roads do not know us anymore.
Peace is no longer settled for us.

I came here –
An escape from the dust of war.
I never thought I would travel between the clouds,
And my feet on my heart
returned me ruin
ruin
ruin

Gaelic

Aisling is a dream in another language,
Is love
without fear,
without limits.
It lights me up,
And then leaves me
aching for forever.

Ember under the Ash

I loved you with some of me
But when you went
You took all of me

I didn't know that all seasons will follow you
and turn all my years into faces without features

I went to the
bar
cabaret
pub
church
synagogue
mosque
listened to the old hymns which might tame the sadness
that lives with me
Wound that breathes from my lung

i scream
run
crawl
jump
drink
pray
dance
sing
laugh

cry
beseech
entreat

I have wept too much, more than I should
Please return my oblivion to me

God has no Religion

God has no bell nor minaret
God has The Symphony of Love
God is love
And love in the air.

Don't look for him in your books,
Neither Christianity
nor Islam
Neither Hinduism
nor Judaism...

Don't use these words as titles for me or them,
He said we are all beyond words –
No more words.
No more terms.
Hear only love within silence

When you see the one
Who loves you
Leave this world,
Forget it,
Leave your heart,
Live in such a way that should you ever release...
Leave these differences.
Be with me,
He will open all the gates to you

Your religion
Sees God in sword and blood
I sense him
In a song
In a sky
In the sea
In the green fields
In your blue eyes

Religion is gathering of Lovers.
There is no black,
no white,
no low,
no high,

Religion is when I love you
And you love me, without names without colours

Religion is when I'm warm sun in your windy day
And you are light moon in my dark night

O baby
I'm thirsty for your light
I'm so 'religious'
I can't be without you...
Why don't you say it too?

DRUG

Learn poetry
This is no more healing drug than swimming in the words

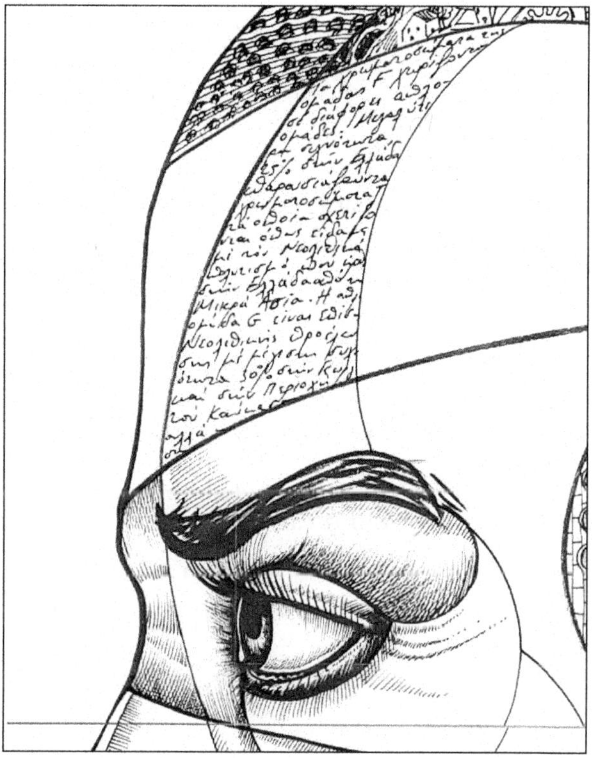

Letter to Trump

Write down
I'm Muslim.
I'm from Sumerians who taught your ancestors to write.
Who taught me the pride of the sun
Long before I could read.

Write down
I'm Muslim.
I'm from Hammurabi
Who taught America what is law and urban civilization.
You, who were neither well-bred, nor well-born!

Write down
I'm Muslim.
My roots were entrenched before the birth of time.
I'm from the Land of Oil:
Black gold, which is your dream to steal.

Write down
I'm Muslim.
You left nothing for us
But these rocks.
So will your state take them
As it has been foretold?

Therefore:
Write down

I'm Muslim.
Nor do I encroach.

But if I become angry,
The usurper's flesh will be my food.
Beware.
Beware
Of my anger.

Write down
I'm Muslim.
I'm the hot sun in a desert of magic you cannot get
In your palaces of gold.

Write down
I'm Muslim
From the chocolate brown of my skin.
From my Mesopotamian civilization your armies invaded
And left empty handed

Write down
I'm Muslim.

MAKING BLOOD

Everyone has a poem
And I am in the middle of the poem
A poem can gulp us down, for years, ages,
I can't walk out somewhere else.

How can I stop this bleeding ?

The Poet and Chuinn

From the country that taught me how to scatter,
Who turned my tears into rain.
From there,
I travelled with Wilson to see Chuinn,
The One of the Hundred Battles,
The victor who defeated lovers and left them to praise him.
He is a Celtic tiger
Derived from wisdom, reason, intelligence.
Wilson said, "He will guide you to a port of safety,
And, will provide justice for all,
With commitment to saving our birds.
And will help you to fulfil your dream of being free."

Chuinn's job is to release birds from a fisherman's mouth.
He is like a dream but I cannot be a dreamer
drunk with thirst,
I dream of being with him.
Like a pebble longing for the riverbank.
Like a bird longing for the wind
I sing to him,
Write, draw, cry, dance...
But round his throne he keeps a crowd of disciples, slave girls, homeless, victims
He calls me a drowning man, and asks, "Why have a dream with my glories?"
I say, "Courage, Sire, I am a poet,
And poets cannot be tamed."

He smiles, and makes a sign to his executioner.
So,
teach this crazy poet how to write his last poem
by bisecting his heart and sewing it back together and then beheading him.

Then, full stop.

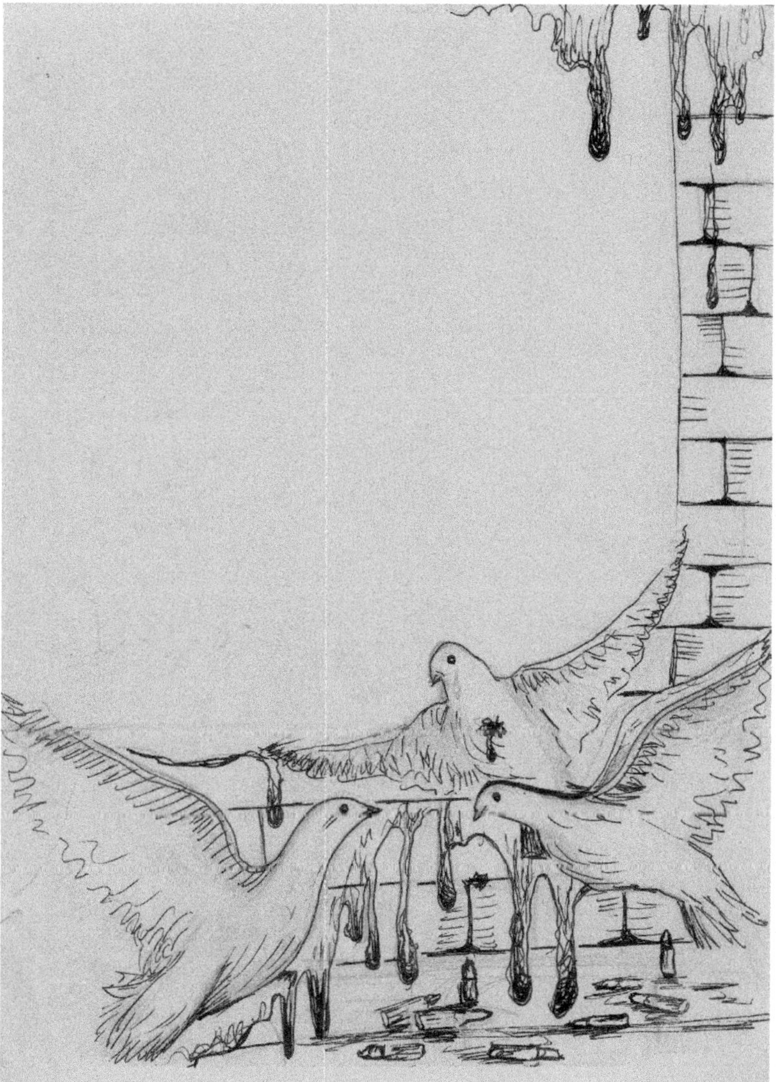

Message from the Author

I'm very pleased that my poetry can be published as a book to support three projects in England, because of their important work for humanitarian support. There are many people that need help and this is what they do. Therefore, I'm willing to support them. It is my love to help people as much as I can; it makes me feel like a better person. I want to help the community, because I believe volunteering makes a difference in the lives of everyone who participates.

When I was in Iraq I had a good salary and was able to support disadvantaged people and protect women's rights. I am now seeking asylum in the UK but I cannot earn money or have a job because I have no right to work yet. I'm glad that I have written a poetry book which, I hope, will raise some funding for these small charities and organizations that support refugees and asylum seekers. They aim to give individuals the opportunity to participate positively, and to be themselves again after they have lost hope and their homeland.

When you buy this book, the funds raised will help to support asylum seekers, and alleviate stress and anxiety. I hope my poetry inspires you to do one small thing to diminish oppression.

All proceeds from the sale of this book will be shared between the Baobab Women's Project, Greater Lincolnshire Area of Sanctuary, and the Destitution Fund of the Leicester City of Sanctuary.

Baobab Women's Project

Greater Lincolnshire Area of Sanctuary

Leicester City of Sanctuary

Cover design by London Tags

LONDON tags
MULTIMEDIA PRODUCTION

21 Malvern Road London NW6 5PS
020 7604 3052 | 079 4489 9990
www.londonTags.com | info@londonTags.com

Lightning Source UK Ltd.
Milton Keynes UK
UKOW01f0636150218
317920UK00002B/91/P

9 780955 493997